GUATEMALA

CONTENTS

COUNTRY OVERVIEW: GUATEMALA AT A GLANCE

History and Government

For much of its post-contact history, Guatemala was a colonial state, in which kingdoms and the church were the sole sources of legitimate power. The compensation for colonial administrators was in the form of land grants and control over the people living on those lands. Colonial administrators were expected to collect taxes on behalf of kingdoms, and the expectation was that a portion of the taxes collected would be used by the administrator for personal expenses.

Guatemala gained independence from Spanish colonial rule on September 15, 1821. During the second half of the 20th century, Guatemala experienced a variety of military and civilian governments, as well as a 36-year guerrilla war, which led to the massacre of more than 200,000 people and created approximately 1 million refugees. Ninety-two percent of the deaths were attributed to the Guatemalan military. In 1996, the government signed a peace agreement formally ending the conflict. Although the signing of the peace accord ended the internal armed conflict, the causes of the war are deeply rooted and tenaciously resistant. Former combatants and perpetrators of the massacres often live side by side with the victims and their families. A continued high level of violence and crime is an unfortunate part of the ongoing struggle of all Guatemalans to recover from the trauma of war.

Guatemala is a constitutional, democratic republic. The current constitution became effective in January 1986. It was suspended by President Jorge Serrano from May 1993 until his ousting in June of that year. The executive branch consists of the president and vice president, elected through a popular vote every four years, and cabinet members appointed by the president. There is a unicameral congress; members are elected by popular vote every four years. Supreme Court members, who serve five-year terms, are appointed by the president of Guatemala and the outgoing president of the court. Suffrage is universal for Guatemalans over the age of 18, excluding soldiers on active duty in the armed services. The country is divided into 22 departments.

Guatemala held general elections in November of 2011 and chose a new president, congress, and municipal authorities. The election process was carried out peacefully and transparently and President Otto Perez Molina took office on January 14, 2012. New municipal governments have also taken office at the local level.

Economy

Agriculture is one of the largest economic sectors and accounts for approximately 60 percent of the work force, 25 percent of the gross domestic product, and 30 percent of exports. Wealthy farmers, using the best agricultural land, produce traditional exports: coffee, bananas, cardamom, cotton, beef, and sugar. Subsistence farmers work on small plots of marginal land, mainly producing beans and corn for local consumption. A quickly expanding nontraditional sector produces and exports non-indigenous fruits, vegetables, ornamental plants, and flowers.

Manufacturing and construction account for one-fifth of gross domestic product. Assuming office in January 1996, then-President Arzu worked to implement a program of economic liberalization and political modernization. The signing of the peace accords in December 1996 removed a major obstacle to foreign investment. Remaining challenges include increasing government revenues, tax collection, negotiating further assistance from international donors, and increasing the efficiency and transparency of both government and private financial operations. Recent administrations have all tried to promote more economic growth and, at the same time, increase public health and educations services.

Guatemala also ratified the Central America Free Trade Agreement (CAFTA-DR) in March 2005, and the agreement went into effect on July 1, 2006. This agreement eliminated customs tariffs on as many categories of goods as possible, opened services sectors, and created more enforceable rules across various market sectors. It also seeks to provide protection for internationally recognized labor rights and environmental standards.

People and Culture

Guatemala straddles the frontier between traditional village cultures and a national culture. Urban populations and communities in the east or *oriente* tend to be dominated by Spanish-speaking *ladinos* (the term used for people whose primary cultural identification is as non-Indian) and rural populations in the western highlands consist mainly of indigenous peoples, including *Quiché, Q'eqchi', Kaqchikel, Mam, Tz'utujil*, and more than 15 other ethnic groups. At the risk of greatly over-simplifying extremely complex phenomena, Guatemalan village culture tends to be organized along lines of familial and marriage relationships. Outsiders, even those with the best of intentions, tend to be viewed by villagers with suspicion. The Guatemalan village culture tends to focus on those aspects of life that reinforce the community's understanding of its shared history, and there is the tendency to idealize the past. In general, Guatemalan villagers consider the problems they confront to be the result of outside forces or the consequence of villagers' failure to follow local cultural traditions. The national culture, toward which the country is gradually moving, is organized along the lines of geographic residence, encompassing successively larger administrative units, culminating in the idea of the nation itself. Within the national culture, there is the belief that local communities are inherently the organizational unit best able to resolve local problems. The reconciliation of these two world views is one of the major challenges that Guatemala faces.

Environment

Guatemala possesses a striking topography and a wide range of climates—from hot, low-lying rainforests to cold mountains reaching 4,220 meters in elevation. The country is home to a wealth of biodiversity and natural beauty, which make it a popular tourist destination. You will find cloud forests echoing with the calls of howler monkeys; crisp, scenic crater lakes; mangroves and beaches; and dusty deserts, all within a country about the size of Tennessee. There is the potential for hurricanes, tropical storms, floods, volcanic activity, and landslides.

Guatemala lies at the convergence of three tectonic plates and experiences frequent seismic activity, mostly small tremors. The last major earthquake occurred in 1976. There are a number of volcanoes in Guatemala. Many are dormant; however, *Volcán Pacaya* and *Volcán de Fuego*, located near the capital city, erupt with some frequency, though most eruptions are more scenic than damaging.

RESOURCES FOR FURTHER INFORMATION

Following is a list of websites for additional information about the Peace Corps and Guatemala and to connect you to returned Volunteers and other invitees. Please keep in mind that although we try to make sure all these links are active and current, we cannot guarantee it. If you do not have access to the Internet, visit your local library. Libraries offer free Internet usage and often let you print information to take home.

A note of caution: As you surf the Internet, be aware that you may find bulletin boards and chat rooms in which people are free to express opinions about the Peace Corps based on their own experience, including comments by those who were unhappy with their choice to serve in the Peace Corps. These opinions are not those of the Peace Corps or the U.S. government, and we hope you will keep in mind that no two people experience their service in the same way.

General Information About Guatemala

www.countrywatch.com/

On this site, you can learn anything from what time it is in the capital of Guatemala to how to convert from the dollar to the Guatemala Quetzal. Just click on Guatemala and go from there.

www.lonelyplanet.com/destinations

Visit this site for general travel advice about almost any country in the world.

www.state.gov

The State Department's website issues background notes periodically about countries around the world. Find Guatemala and learn more about its social and political history. You can also go to the site's international travel section to check on conditions that may affect your safety.

www.psr.keele.ac.uk/official.htm

This includes links to all the official sites for governments worldwide.

www.geography.about.com/library/maps/blindex.htm

This online world atlas includes maps and geographical information, and each country page contains links to other sites, such as the Library of Congress, that contain comprehensive historical, social, and political background.

www.cyberschoolbus.un.org/infonation/info.asp

This United Nations site allows you to search for statistical information for member states of the U.N.

www.worldinformation.com

This site provides an additional source of current and historical information about countries around the world.

Connect With Returned Volunteers and Other Invitees

www.rpcv.org

This is the site of the National Peace Corps Association, made up of returned Volunteers. On this site you can find links to all the Web pages of the "Friends of" groups for most countries of service, comprised of former Volunteers who served in those countries. There are also regional groups that frequently get together for social events and local volunteer activities.

This site is hosted by a group of returned Volunteer writers. It is a monthly online publication of essays and Volunteer accounts of their Peace Corps service.

Online Articles/Current News Sites About Guatemala

Prensa Libre: www.prensalibre.com (in Spanish)

Siglo Veintiuno: www.sigloxxi.com (in Spanish)

La Hora: www.lahora.com.gt (in Spanish)

El Periódico: www.elperiodico.com.gt (in Spanish)

The Revue: www.revuemag.com/home/ (In English)

Recommended Books

1. Archdiocese of Guatemala. *Guatemala: Never Again!* Trans. Thomas Quigley. Orbis Books (1999)

2. Victor Montejo. *Voices from Exile: Violence and Survival in Modern Maya History.* University of Oklahoma Press (1999)

3. Victor Perera and Daniel Chauche (Photographer). *Unfinished Conquest: The Guatemalan Tragedy.* University of California Press (1995)

Books About the History of the Peace Corps
1. Hoffman, Elizabeth Cobbs. *All You Need is Love: The Peace Corps and the Spirit of the 1960s.* Cambridge, Mass.: Harvard University Press, 2000.

2. Rice, Gerald T. *The Bold Experiment: JFK's Peace Corps.* Notre Dame, Ind.: University of Notre Dame Press, 1985.

3. Stossel, Scott. *Sarge: The Life and Times of Sargent Shriver.* Washington, D.C.: Smithsonian Institution Press, 2004.

4. Meisler, Stanley. *When the World Calls: The Inside Story of the Peace Corps and its First 50 Years.* Boston, Mass.: Beacon Press, 2011.

Books on the Volunteer Experience

1. Dirlam, Sharon. *Beyond Siberia: Two Years in a Forgotten Place.* Santa Barbara, Calif.: McSeas Books, 2004.

2. Casebolt, Marjorie DeMoss. *Margarita: A Guatemalan Peace Corps Experience.* Gig Harbor, Wash.: Red Apple Publishing, 2000.

3. Erdman, Sarah. *Nine Hills to Nambonkaha: Two Years in the Heart of an African Village.* New York, N.Y.: Picador, 2003.

4. Hessler, Peter. *River Town: Two Years on the Yangtze.* New York, N.Y.: Perennial, 2001.

5.   Kennedy, Geraldine ed. *From the Center of the Earth: Stories out of the Peace Corps*. Santa Monica, Calif.: Clover Park Press, 1991.

6.   Thompsen, Moritz. *Living Poor: A Peace Corps Chronicle*. Seattle, Wash.: University of Washington Press, 1997 (reprint).

LIVING CONDITIONS AND VOLUNTEER LIFESTYLE

Communications

Mail
Few countries in the world offer the level of mail service we consider normal in the United States. Guatemala's mail service is fair, but often unreliable. Mail usually takes at least two weeks to arrive; however, it is common for letters to arrive much later, or never at all. It is recommended that you arrange a system of numbering correspondence with family and friends.

Once you complete training and are assigned to your site you will need to inform family and friends of your mailing address in your community.

Receiving packages can be problematic as packages might be held at the central post office for pickup and customs duties will be your responsibility. Often, the packages are opened or never arrive at all. Experience has shown that small padded envelopes are most likely to arrive intact. Due to U.S. Embassy security regulations, the Peace Corps office in Guatemala is unable to receive any packages or mail for Volunteers.

Telephones
As cellphones are an important tool for Volunteers in terms of safety and security, work, and support, trainees are assigned official cellphones shortly after they arrive to use throughout their service as Volunteers in Guatemala. We strongly discourage you from bringing a cellphone with you from the United States, as it is highly unlikely that your plan will cover Guatemala and the surrounding region.

The organization to which you are assigned (your host agency) may have telephone service at its office; however, that office may be a great distance from where you live. In the more developed cities, residential phone service is available, and there are a few Volunteers who have home phones. Also, most communities have families who rent out their phone for calls.

The Peace Corps office in Guatemala can be reached by direct dialing from the United States. The number is 011-502-7828-2500. Volunteers are not permitted to use telephones at the Peace Corps office in Guatemala to call family and friends unless the call pertains to an emergency and is approved by the country director.

Computer, Internet, and Email Access
Computer and Internet access exists throughout much of Guatemala. Much like the telephone, most Volunteers will be able to use these services locally or during a short trip to a nearby town. Internet cafés can be found in most Guatemalan cities or towns and since connection fees can be high, Peace Corps/Guatemala includes a small stipend for Internet use in your monthly living allowance to help defray the costs. There are also Internet-connected computers at the Peace Corps offices. Many host agencies have Internet-connected computers that you might also be able to access for work-related or personal use.

Many Volunteers do bring laptop computers with them, which they use for work or personal purposes and, via USB modems, most will have access to the Internet. Netbook-style computers, because of their small size and lower cost, are also good options for day-to-day use. Possessing a laptop can be a security concern in Guatemala, since they command high prices on the black market. They can also be damaged or lost and specialized repair services may be expensive or non-existent.

Housing and Site Location

Volunteer housing and site locations vary depending on your project and the type of work you will do. Peace Corps staff members work with your host agency, Volunteers who currently live in the area, and municipal leaders to locate appropriate sites and determine if the living conditions meet selection criteria established by the Peace Corps. In addition, the Peace Corps consults with security staff at the U.S. Embassy to review any pertinent safety concerns that might be present in a geographic area.

Because of the importance of community integration and for your own safety and security, you are **required** to live with a host family for the duration of your Volunteer service. Privacy may at times be scarce, but the experience of sharing day-to-day life with a Guatemalan family will hasten your cultural adaptation, language ability, and will help you appreciate the lifestyle of rural Guatemalan families. Your personal safety will be enhanced when the community sees you as a part of a local family. As this housing policy is a mandatory and non-negotiable requirement, it is important to think about this commitment and your ability to be flexible enough to live with a family in basic conditions, with limited privacy. Married couples are also required to live with a family.

The type of house you live in will depend on what is common in the area. In a city or large town, this will likely be a cement block house with a tin or tile roof and a solid floor. Most will have electricity. Most households in Guatemala have a *pila*—a large cement sink for washing dishes and clothes, with a section for collecting water. In more developed areas, you will likely have plumbing, although service may be intermittent. You may have a flush toilet or use a latrine that is separate from the house.

Volunteers in more rural areas may live in a house of cement or adobe (homemade brick), with a roof of tin, tile, or thatch. Most have solid floors, but in poorer areas some have dirt floors. Electricity is present in almost all areas, even small villages, and some use a generator for a few hours each night. However, power outages are very frequent, especially in rural sites. You may come to rely on candles and lanterns during the evening. Most will have an outside *pila*, but you may find yourself carrying water from a community water source or collecting rainwater to fill it. In some areas, people use a community *pila* or a river for their water source.

Living Allowance and Money Management

Volunteers receive a living allowance adequate to their needs as determined by annual cost-of-living surveys. Volunteers are entirely responsible for managing their personal finances. Living allowances permit Volunteers to live according to the standards of the people with whom they live and work and will be based on local costs, including transport, rent, and food. The principal bank used by Peace Corps/Guatemala is Banco Industrial. Upon arrival in Guatemala, each Volunteer will open a personal checking account with this bank and sign a Power of Attorney form authorizing Peace Corps/Guatemala to make deposits for living allowances and reimbursements as necessary. Prior to leaving Guatemala, each Volunteer must personally close the account after determining that all checks and payments have cleared and must make the necessary arrangements to cover those that have not. For convenience, Volunteers often open a second account at a bank in or near their site. Funds can then be transferred from the Banco Industrial account into a secondary account.

Food and Diet

Most Volunteers enjoy eating the typical food in their community. In towns and cities, you will usually find a greater variety; in poor rural areas, the food choices can be limited. Throughout Guatemala, corn tortillas and black beans are a staple. Other common foods include eggs, rice, chicken soup, and bread delivered from bakeries in larger towns. These foods are eaten daily in most poor areas of Guatemala. The most common fruits and vegetables include tomatoes, onions, avocado, a squash called *huisquil* (chayote in the United

States), bananas, and mangoes (when in season). Papaya and citrus fruits are found in some areas. Chicken or pork tamales are also common, in addition to a sweet rice or corn drink called *atol*.

In more developed areas, you might find a greater variety of food, including more meat (usually chicken) and more fruits and vegetables.

Even in the most rural areas, there are usually small local stores that stock snacks, sodas, and staples. Traditional outdoor markets, where you can find fresh fruits, vegetables, meat, clothing, and household items are open on a regular basis (usually weekly) in central towns and are always open in main cities. In larger cities, you will also find supermarkets, where you can purchase nonperishable items and imported goods. Some Volunteers take advantage of the opportunity to stock up on special foods and cooking items, such as spices, peanut butter, and pasta when visiting larger cities.

Being a vegetarian as a Volunteer is not difficult. In many of the poorer areas, for example, meat is rarely eaten. However, meat is prepared on special occasions and there will likely be situations when meat is offered to you. Many Volunteers have successfully served as vegetarians, and you will need to find appropriate strategies to deal with these situations, depending on your specific circumstances.

Transportation

Guatemala has extensive and relatively cheap transportation in major urban areas and relatively good access in some rural areas. Volunteers often travel around their sites for work activities on foot, in the company of other community members or work colleagues.

For local travel, Volunteers usually ride in vans or "chicken buses" (U.S. school buses painted and outfitted with racks to haul supplies and sometimes animals). In rural areas, you might have a bus that leaves your site once a day, travels to a major city, and returns at night. In other areas, pickup trucks provide transportation to villages on a regular basis instead of a bus. Sometimes, you may arrange for a ride with someone you know who has a car or pickup. For long distances on major routes, there are "Pullmans," which are similar to Greyhound buses and provide a more comfortable and secure ride at a higher fee. Please note that Peace Corps/Guatemala currently has an official shuttle system for transport between the two country offices. Volunteers are required to use this shuttle service if traveling on that route. A schedule will be provided for this service during pre-service training. Volunteers find that the shuttle system is quite convenient for travel.

Geography and Climate

Guatemala is the northernmost and most populous of the Central American republics. More than 14 million people live in an area about the size of Tennessee or Ohio. Guatemala has coastlines on the Pacific and the Caribbean, and it borders Mexico, Belize, Honduras, and El Salvador.

The central highlands are the most densely populated area. Between the highlands and the Pacific lies a narrow plain. The Caribbean lowlands have fertile river valleys. The north of the country contains tropical jungles and protected biospheres.

Temperatures are fairly constant year-round and are most influenced by elevation. In the cattle country of eastern Guatemala and coastal lowlands, temperatures can reach 100 degrees Fahrenheit. In western Guatemala, the highest part of Central America (and location where most Volunteers are placed), the climate is cold, and morning temperatures in December and January are frequently below freezing. In areas of more moderate elevation, the climate is generally cooler in the mornings and evenings, but warm to hot in the afternoons. Average temperatures fluctuate between 50 and 70 F. The most noticeable feature of Guatemala's tropical climate is the seasonal alternation between dry and rainy seasons. From May to October, most parts of the country get rain every day, resulting in lush vegetation and cooler temperatures. During the dry season

(November to April), rain tapers off and most sections of the country get no rain. This results in dry, dusty weather and hotter temperatures.

Social Activities

There are three prominent aspects of rural social life in Guatemala. The first has to do with the religious celebrations of the community and families. Births, confirmations, coming-of-age ceremonies, communions, marriages, and funerals are themes for the celebration of life. Funerals, in particular, are the recognition of the accomplishments and thoughts of the departed.

The second aspect of social life in rural Guatemala centers on the market, which is far more than a place to buy needed goods. The market is the place to meet and visit with people to exchange news and hold discussions.

The third facet of social life is inter-community competition. Winning a soccer game against a neighboring community, or even losing, creates a sense of solidarity and identity. For most Volunteers, getting involved with sporting events and activities is the easiest way to integrate fully into the community.

Professionalism, Dress, and Behavior

In Guatemala, a Peace Corps Volunteer is expected to be a development professional, demonstrating an ongoing commitment to the highest quality of work. It takes most Volunteers a while to get a sense of what constitutes a reasonable personal workload. Some Volunteers may have a busy schedule of activities set up with their counterparts or host agency. Other Volunteers may be in a less structured environment, where they must get to know their community, find various avenues for work, and develop their own schedules. Because of logistical considerations, some routine tasks will take longer to complete in Guatemala than in the United States.

Appropriate dress is very important, since physical appearance makes a personal statement in Guatemala. What constitutes appropriate dress for work will vary depending on the type of work you will be doing. Your volunteer assignment description (VAD) will provide specific guidelines.

In general, the norm is a conservative, neat appearance. Except in tourist areas and a few locations near the coast, men do not wear shorts or sandals. Pants or jeans with a clean button-down shirt, polo, or nice T-shirt are common for work and casual wear. Long hair, piercings, tattoos, or earrings on men are associated with drug dealers and gang members, and thus are not acceptable for Volunteers. Likewise, dreadlocks are not an acceptable hairstyle for Volunteers in Guatemala. Any type of military-style clothing (e.g., camouflage) is strictly prohibited because of association with the civil war. You will be expected to adjust your appearance, if necessary, to accommodate the above standards.

Women in Guatemala tend to take pride in their appearance and "dress up." In indigenous areas, women wear hand-woven traditional dress. In other areas of the country, dress varies depending on the site. In conservative areas and small villages, you are likely to see women wearing mid-length dresses, or a skirt with a blouse or T-shirt. In towns and more modern areas, it is common to see women in pants or jeans, and you might see women dressed in a manner that Americans might consider flashy. Female Volunteers are not expected to adopt traditional dress or dress like the women in their community; however, your attire should reflect your status as a professional. Female Volunteers usually wear dresses, skirts, pants, or jeans, with short-sleeved or modest sleeveless blouses in hotter climates. Shorts, bare shoulders, and tank tops should be avoided except while on vacation in tourist areas. For assignments that require a lot of hiking or field work, pants are most appropriate. It is important to note that tight or revealing clothing for women could attract negative attention. Volunteers are expected to dress conservatively.

The Peace Corps has a zero-tolerance policy on the use of illegal drugs, including marijuana. Drug use is illegal in Guatemala, and puts both the safety of the Volunteer and the image of the Peace Corps at great risk. Use of illegal drugs will result in immediate separation from the Peace Corps. There are absolutely no exceptions.

Volunteers are "on duty" representing Peace Corps 24 hours a day, seven days a week, even while relaxing on weekends or on vacation. Your use of alcohol, relationships with Guatemalans and other Volunteers, and your general lifestyle are constantly under observation by the community around you and by other Americans who may be in the country as tourists or on private business. This can, at times, feel like a restriction on your personal liberties. If you do not feel comfortable with such a responsibility, and are not willing to make any necessary adjustments to your lifestyle, then it would be best not to accept this invitation to serve.

Peace Corps/Guatemala believes in the commitment of Volunteers to their project, and the organizations and community members with whom they work. We expect all Volunteers to dedicate their time and efforts to the Guatemalans they serve in their respective project locations. Vacation time and tourism should be utilized as a compliment to your service, not a primary focus. Vacation leave provides Volunteers with the opportunity to increase their understanding of the host country and region, while allowing time for rest and relaxation. Volunteers accrue two days of annual leave for each month of service. Because Volunteers are deemed to be on duty at all times, all Volunteer leave is computed in terms of calendar days rather than workdays. Vacation should be taken at appropriate times (i.e., with respect to local work priorities), in coordination with your counterparts, and approved by your project manager.

Personal Safety

More detailed information about the Peace Corps' approach to safety is contained in the "Health Care and Safety" chapter, but it is an important issue and cannot be overemphasized. As stated in the *Volunteer Handbook,* becoming a Peace Corps Volunteer entails certain safety risks. Living and traveling in an unfamiliar environment (oftentimes alone), having a limited understanding of local language and culture, and being perceived as well-off are some of the factors that can put a Volunteer at risk. Many Volunteers experience varying degrees of unwanted attention and harassment. Petty thefts and burglaries are not uncommon, and incidents of physical and sexual assault do occur, although most Guatemala Volunteers complete their two years of service without incident. The Peace Corps has established procedures and policies designed to help you reduce your risks and enhance your safety and security. These procedures and policies, in addition to safety training, will be provided once you arrive in Guatemala. Using these tools, you are expected to take responsibility for your safety and well-being.

Each staff member at the Peace Corps is committed to providing Volunteers with the support they need to successfully meet the challenges they will face to have a safe, healthy, and productive service. We encourage Volunteers and families to look at our safety and security information on the Peace Corps website at www.peacecorps.gov/safety.

Messages about Volunteer health and Volunteer safety are included. There is a section titled "Safety and Security in Depth." Among topics addressed are the risks of serving as a Volunteer, posts' safety support systems, and emergency planning and communications.

Rewards and Frustrations

Both the rewards and frustrations of service in Guatemala seem to come mostly from the differences between U.S. and Guatemalan culture. In the United States, the culture emphasizes "action" or "doing," in which a person's value to society is assessed primarily in terms of what he or she is able to achieve over the course of a lifetime. In Guatemala, the culture emphasizes "being," where social value is a function of affiliation and group solidarity. Some Volunteers have a difficult time appreciating the importance of simply spending time with associates and community members to establish trust based on interpersonal relationships. Most agencies to which Volunteers are assigned have little cultural understanding of the U.S. ethic of volunteerism, and they may have a limited understanding of what kind of support and supervision Volunteers need to feel productive. The rewards, particularly for self-starters with high energy, are ample opportunities to make a measurable difference in the lives of the people served.

PEACE CORPS TRAINING

Overview of Pre-Service Training

The Peace Corps office is located in Santa Lucia Milpas Altas, in the department of Sacatepéquez. This is a small town settled along the road that runs between Antigua and Guatemala City. Pre-service training consists of nine and a half weeks of hands-on activities to help you develop and practice the skills you will need as a Volunteer. In this first part of training, you will focus on developing skills in language, culture, health, safety and security, and basic technical skills. After being in site for several months, you will return to the Peace Corps office for an additional two weeks of training, primarily in your technical area. Our training philosophy can be summed up by the phrase: Learning by doing. There will be some classroom work and some readings, but most of the training will be in your training community, using methods and materials available to the people and communities with whom you will be working.

Pre-service training provides the opportunity for you to continue to explore your commitment to service and understand what is expected of Volunteers who serve in Guatemala. In order to swear in as a Volunteer, you will need to demonstrate your ability to successfully work in development through your acquisition of local language, your application of technical, cultural, safety, and health skills, as well as through professionalism and integration into your Guatemalan host community. Peace Corps staff will provide you with both verbal and written feedback throughout the pre-service training process to help you understand your progress toward becoming a Peace Corps Volunteer.

Technical Training

Technical training will prepare you to work in Guatemala by building on the skills you already have and helping you develop new skills in a manner appropriate to the needs of the country. The Peace Corps staff, Guatemalan experts, and current Volunteers will conduct the training program. Training places great emphasis on learning how to transfer the skills you have to the community in which you will serve as a Volunteer.

Technical training will include sessions on the general economic and political environment in Guatemala and strategies for working within such a framework. You will review your technical sector goals and will meet with the Guatemala agencies and organizations that invited the Peace Corps to assist them. You will be supported and evaluated throughout the training to build the confidence and skills you need to undertake your project activities and be a productive member of your community.

After your first few months in site, you will return to the Peace Corps office to receive additional technical training based on priorities you have identified through a community diagnostic assessment. Your technical skills will build upon what you already know and be geared toward real-world application.

Language Training

As a Peace Corps Volunteer, you will find that language skills are critical to personal and professional satisfaction during your service. These skills are essential for your job performance, community integration, personal adaptation to new surroundings, and for your safety and security. Therefore, language training is at the heart of the training program. You must successfully meet minimum language requirements to complete training and become a Volunteer. Guatemala language instructors teach formal language classes five days a week in small groups of four to five people. Language training is also integrated in the health, culture, and technical components of training.

Your language training will incorporate a community-based approach. In addition to classroom time, you will be given assignments to work on outside of the classroom and with your host family. The goal is to get you to a point of basic social communication skills so you can practice and develop language skills further once you are at your site. Prior to being sworn in as a Volunteer, you will work on strategies to continue language studies during your service.

If you come to Guatemala with an advanced level of Spanish you will receive several weeks of training in Guatemalan expressions and culture and then be given work assignments to carry out in your training community. Many advanced speakers want to continue perfecting their Spanish in structured language activities like their colleagues who are starting at a lower level; however, Peace Corps language training is designed to assist trainees in reaching the language level necessary to begin work. Those who are tested at a more advanced Spanish level will begin more substantive work in their training communities earlier than trainees who need more language training.

Near the end of pre-service training, all Volunteers will also receive a half-day orientation to Mayan languages. For Volunteers who live in communities where Mayan languages are spoken, they may apply to the Mayan language program where a local language instructor will be identified for private or small group tutoring in the local language.

Cross-Cultural Training

As part of your pre-service training, you will live with a Guatemalan host family. This experience is designed to ease your transition to life at your site. Families go through an orientation conducted by Peace Corps staff to explain the purpose of pre-service training and to assist them in helping you adapt to living in Guatemala. Many Volunteers form strong and lasting friendships with their host families.

Cross-cultural and community development training will help you improve your communication skills and understand your role as a facilitator of development. You will be exposed to topics such as community mobilization, conflict resolution, gender and development, non-formal and adult education strategies, and local political structures.

Aside from specific cross-cultural training sessions, theories and skills will be integrated and reinforced in all other aspects of your training in order to help you to understand how to apply the concepts within a community-based context. Peace Corps staff and Volunteers, host families, and community members will all provide you feedback on ways to successfully adapt to and understand the intricacies of Volunteer work in Guatemala.

Health Training

During pre-service training, you will be given basic medical training and information. You will be expected to practice preventive health care and to take responsibility for your own health by adhering to all medical policies. Trainees are required to attend all medical sessions. The topics include preventive health measures and minor and major medical issues that you might encounter while in Guatemala. Nutrition, mental health, setting up a safe living compound, and how to avoid HIV/AIDS and other sexually transmitted infections (STIs) are also covered.

These sessions are an important part of your training. Your collaboration with us in this partnership is the most important aspect. Your health will depend on how well you assume personal responsibility for your own well-being. You will need to make a concerted effort to institute healthful practices into your daily routine. It is our goal to make you aware of the physical, environmental, and social factors that affect your health while in Guatemala. Peace Corps/Guatemala's medical sessions have been designed to provide the support, reinforcement, and development of your skills for health maintenance and disease prevention.

Safety Training

During the safety training sessions, you will learn how to adopt a lifestyle that reduces your risks at home, at work, and during your travels. You will also learn appropriate, effective strategies for coping with unwanted attention and about your individual responsibility for promoting safety throughout your service.

After receiving classroom sessions on safety, you will put the skills into practice throughout your host family stay, while using local transportation, and during your work in the community. Peace Corps staff and your host family will provide you with guidance and feedback throughout training to help you develop reflexes, behaviors, and habits that can help you reduce risk.

Additional Trainings during Volunteer Service

In its commitment to institutionalize quality training, the Peace Corps has implemented a training system that provides Volunteers with continual opportunities to examine their commitment to Peace Corps service while increasing their technical and cross-cultural skills. During service, there are usually three training events. The titles and objectives for those trainings are as follows:

- In-service training: *Provides an opportunity for Volunteers to upgrade their technical, language, and project development skills while sharing their experiences and reaffirming their commitment after having served for three to six months.*

- Midterm conference (done in conjunction with technical sector in-service): *Assists Volunteers in reviewing their first year, reassessing their personal and project objectives, and planning for their second year of service.*

- Close-of-service conference: *Prepares Volunteers for the future after Peace Corps service and reviews their respective projects and personal experiences.*

The number, length, and design of these trainings are adapted to country-specific needs and conditions. The key to the training system is that training events are integrated and interrelated, from the pre-departure orientation through the end of your service, and are planned, implemented, and evaluated cooperatively by the training staff, Peace Corps staff, and Volunteers.

YOUR HEALTH CARE AND
SAFETY IN GUATEMALA

The Peace Corps' highest priority is maintaining the good health and safety of every Volunteer. Peace Corps medical programs emphasize the preventive, rather than the curative, approach to disease. The Peace Corps in Guatemala maintains two clinics with full-time medical officers, who take care of Volunteers' primary health care needs. Additional medical services, such as testing and basic treatment, are also available in Guatemala at local hospitals. If you become seriously ill, you will be transported either to an American-standard medical facility in the region or to the United States.

Health Issues in Guatemala

Outside of major cities, the national health care infrastructure is based mainly on rural clinics, supported by some hospitals. The role of clinics, other than diagnosing endemic health problems and coordinating the training of midwives, is to refer complicated cases to service providers in the larger cities. In many areas of Guatemala, health problems associated with poverty such as malnutrition, water- and food-borne illnesses, tuberculosis, and parasitic infestations are fairly common. Malaria, dengue fever, and Chagas disease are also present. Most health problems in Guatemala can be avoided by consistently using preventive measures.

Helping You Stay Healthy

The Peace Corps will provide you with all the necessary vaccinations, medications, and information to stay healthy. Upon your arrival in Guatemala, you will receive a medical handbook. At the end of training, you will receive a medical kit with supplies to take care of mild illnesses and first aid needs. The contents of the kit are listed later in this chapter.

During pre-service training, you will have access to basic medical supplies through the medical officer. However, you will be responsible for your own supply of prescription drugs and any other specific medical supplies you require, as the Peace Corps will not order these items during training. Please bring a three-month supply of any prescription drugs you use, since they may not be available here and it may take several months for shipments to arrive.

You will have physical examinations at a mid-service conference and at the end of your service. If you develop a serious medical problem during your service, the medical officer in Guatemala will consult with the Office of Medical Services in Washington, D.C. If it is determined that your condition cannot be treated in Guatemala, you may be sent out of the country for further evaluation and care.

Maintaining Your Health

As a Volunteer, you must accept considerable responsibility for your own health. Proper precautions will significantly reduce your risk of serious illness or injury. The adage "An ounce of prevention …" becomes extremely important in areas where diagnostic and treatment facilities are not up to the standards of the United States. The most important of your responsibilities in Guatemala is to take the following preventive measures:

- Compliance with malaria prophylaxis. Failure to take malaria prophylaxis may result in significant illness and possible termination of service.
- For all bites from warm-blooded animals, you should assume the animal is rabid, inform the medical officer, and come into the office for rabies prophylaxis.
- If sexually active, comply with safe sex practices, including the use of condoms for all sexual activity.
- Use an effective method of contraception if sexually active.

- Do not wait until a medical problem becomes critical before seeking treatment.
- Adhere to food and water preparation practices.
- Understand and follow Peace Corps policies relating to drug use (zero tolerance) and alcohol consumption (use in moderation).

Many illnesses that affect Volunteers worldwide are entirely preventable if proper food and water precautions are taken. These illnesses include food poisoning, parasitic infections, hepatitis A, dysentery, Guinea worms, tapeworms, and typhoid fever. Your medical officer will discuss specific standards for water and food preparation in Guatemala during pre-service training.

Abstinence is the only certain choice for preventing infection with HIV and other sexually transmitted infections. You are taking risks if you choose to be sexually active. To lessen risk, use a condom every time you have sex. Whether your partner is a host country citizen, a fellow Volunteer, or anyone else, do not assume this person is free of HIV/AIDS or other STIs. You will receive more information from the medical officer about this important issue.

Volunteers are expected to adhere to an effective means of birth control to prevent an unplanned pregnancy. Your medical officer can help you decide on the most appropriate method to suit your individual needs. Contraceptive methods are available without charge from the medical officer.

It is critical to your health that you promptly report to the medical office or other designated facility for scheduled immunizations, and that you let the medical officer know immediately of significant illnesses and injuries.

Women's Health Information

Pregnancy is treated in the same manner as other Volunteer health conditions that require medical attention but also have programmatic ramifications. The Peace Corps is responsible for determining the medical risk and the availability of appropriate medical care if the Volunteer remains in-country. Given the circumstances under which Volunteers live and work in Peace Corps countries, it is rare that the Peace Corps' medical and programmatic standards for continued service during pregnancy can be met.

If feminine hygiene products are not available for you to purchase on the local market, the Peace Corps medical officer in Guatemala will provide them. If you require a specific product, please bring a three-month supply with you.

Your Peace Corps Medical Kit

The Peace Corps medical officer will provide you with a kit that contains basic items necessary to prevent and treat illnesses that may occur during service. Kit items can be periodically restocked at the medical office.

Medical Kit Contents

Ace bandages

Adhesive tape

American Red Cross First Aid & Safety Handbook

Antacid tablets (Tums)

Antibiotic ointment (Bacitracin/Neomycin/Polymycin B)

Antiseptic antimicrobial skin cleaner (Hibiclens)

Band-Aids

Butterfly closures

Calamine lotion

Cepacol lozenges

Condoms

Dental floss

Diphenhydramine HCL 25 mg (Benadryl)

Insect repellent stick (Cutter's)

Iodine tablets (for water purification)

Lip balm (Chapstick)

Oral rehydration salts

Oral thermometer (Fahrenheit)

Pseudoephedrine HCL 30 mg (Sudafed)

Robitussin-DM lozenges (for cough)

Scissors

Sterile gauze pads

Tetrahydrozaline eyedrops (Visine)

Tinactin (antifungal cream)

Tweezers

Before You Leave: A Medical Checklist

If there has been any change in your health—physical, mental, or dental—since you submitted your examination reports to the Peace Corps, you must immediately notify the Office of Medical Services. Failure to disclose new illnesses, injuries, allergies, or pregnancy can endanger your health and may jeopardize your eligibility to serve.

If your dental exam was done more than a year ago, or if your physical exam is more than two years old, contact the Office of Medical Services to find out whether you need to update your records. If your dentist or Peace Corps dental consultant has recommended that you undergo dental treatment or repair, you must complete that work and make sure your dentist sends requested confirmation reports or X-rays to the Office of Medical Services.

If you wish to avoid having duplicate vaccinations, contact your physician's office to obtain a copy of your immunization record and bring it to your pre-departure orientation. If you have any immunizations prior to Peace Corps service, the Peace Corps cannot reimburse you for the cost. The Peace Corps will provide all the immunizations necessary for your overseas assignment, either at your pre-departure orientation or shortly after you arrive in Guatemala. You do not need to begin taking malaria medication prior to departure.

Bring a three-month supply of any prescription or over-the-counter medication you use on a regular basis, including birth control pills. Although the Peace Corps cannot reimburse you for this three-month supply, it will order refills during your service. While awaiting shipment—which can take several months—you will be dependent on your own medication supply. The Peace Corps will not pay for herbal or nonprescribed medications, such as St. John's wort, glucosamine, selenium, or antioxidant supplements.

You are encouraged to bring copies of medical prescriptions signed by your physician. This is not a requirement, but they might come in handy if you are questioned in transit about carrying a three-month supply of prescription drugs.

If you wear eyeglasses, bring two pairs with you—a pair and a spare. If a pair breaks, the Peace Corps will replace them, using the information your doctor in the United States provided on the eyeglasses form during your examination. The Peace Corps discourages you from using contact lenses during your service to reduce your risk of developing a serious infection or other eye disease. Most Peace Corps countries do not have appropriate water and sanitation to support eye care with the use of contact lenses. The Peace Corps will not supply or replace contact lenses or associated solutions unless an ophthalmologist has recommended their use for a specific medical condition and the Peace Corps' Office of Medical Services has given approval.

If you are eligible for Medicare, are over 50 years of age, or have a health condition that may restrict your future participation in health care plans, you may wish to consult an insurance specialist about unique coverage needs before your departure. The Peace Corps will provide all necessary health care from the time you leave for your pre-departure orientation until you complete your service. When you finish, you will be entitled to the post-service health care benefits described in the Peace Corps *Volunteer Handbook*. You may wish to consider keeping an existing health plan in effect during your service if you think age or pre-existing conditions might prevent you from re-enrolling in your current plan when you return home.

Safety and Security—Our Partnership

Serving as a Volunteer overseas entails certain safety and security risks. Living and traveling in an unfamiliar environment, a limited understanding of the local language and culture, and the perception of being a wealthy American are some of the factors that can put a Volunteer at risk. Property theft and burglaries are not uncommon. Incidents of physical and sexual assault do occur, although almost all Volunteers complete their two years of service without serious personal safety problems.

Beyond knowing that Peace Corps approaches safety and security as a partnership with you, it might be helpful to see how this partnership works. Peace Corps has policies, procedures, and training in place to promote your safety. We depend on you to follow those policies and to put into practice what you have learned. An example of how this works in practice—in this case to help manage the risk of burglary—is:

- Peace Corps assesses the security environment where you will live and work
- Peace Corps inspects and evaluates the family and house where you will live according to established security criteria
- Peace Corps provides you with resources to take measures such as installing new locks
- Peace Corps ensures you are welcomed by host country authorities in your new community
- Peace Corps responds to security concerns that you raise
- You lock your doors and windows
- You adopt a lifestyle appropriate to the community where you live
- You get to know neighbors
- You decide if purchasing personal articles insurance is appropriate for you
- You don't change residence before being authorized by Peace Corps
- You communicate any safety concerns to Peace Corps staff

This *Welcome Book* contains sections on: Living Conditions and Volunteer Lifestyle; Peace Corps Training; and Your Health Care and Safety that all include important safety and security information to help you understand this partnership. The Peace Corps makes every effort to give Volunteers the tools they need to function in the safest way possible, because working to maximize the safety and security of Volunteers is our highest priority. Not only do we provide you with training and tools to prepare for the unexpected, but we teach you to identify, reduce, and manage the risks you may encounter.

Factors that Contribute to Volunteer Risk

There are several factors that can heighten a Volunteer's risk, many of which are within the Volunteer's control. By far the most common crime that Volunteers experience is theft. Thefts often occur when Volunteers are away from their sites, in crowded locations (such as markets or on public transportation), and when leaving items unattended.

Before you depart for Guatemala there are several measures you can take to reduce your risk:

o   Leave valuable objects in the U.S.

o   Leave copies of important documents and account numbers with someone you trust in the U.S.

o   Purchase a hidden money pouch or *"dummy"* wallet as a decoy

o   Purchase personal articles insurance

After you arrive in Guatemala, you will receive more detailed information about common crimes, factors that contribute to Volunteer risk, and local strategies to reduce that risk. For example, Volunteers in Guatemala learn to:

- Choose safe routes and times for travel, and travel with someone trusted by the community whenever possible
- Make sure one's personal appearance is respectful of local customs
- Avoid high-crime areas
- Know the local language to get help in an emergency
- Make friends with local people who are respected in the community
- Limit alcohol consumption

As you can see from this list, you must be willing to work hard and adapt your lifestyle to minimize the potential for being a target for crime. As with anywhere in the world, crime does exist in Guatemala. You can reduce your risk by avoiding situations that place you at risk and by taking precautions. Crime at the village or town level is less frequent than in the large cities; people know each other and generally are less likely to steal from their neighbors. Tourist attractions in large towns are favorite worksites for pickpockets.

The following are other security concerns in Guatemala of which you should be aware:

- The percentage of the population that is armed is high due to the carryover from the civil war that ended in 1996.
- In villages and small towns, citizens frequently take the law into their own hands, dispensing community justice. If you are even suspected of posing a threat to public safety, the consequences can be potentially dangerous.
- Nonessential travel should be kept to a minimum.
- Do not resist robbers. Nothing you own is worth being injured or killed.
- Avoid being out after dark.

While whistles and exclamations may be fairly common on the street, this behavior can be reduced if you dress conservatively, abide by local cultural norms, and respond according to the training you will receive.

Staying Safe: Don't Be a Target for Crime

You must be prepared to take on a large degree of responsibility for your own safety. You can make yourself less of a target, ensure that your home is secure, and develop relationships in your community that will make you an unlikely victim of crime. While the factors that contribute to your risk in Guatemala may be different, in many ways you can do what you would do if you moved to a new city anywhere: Be cautious, check things out, ask questions, learn about your neighborhood, know where the more risky locations are, use common sense, and be aware. You can reduce your vulnerability to crime by integrating into your community, learning the local language, acting responsibly, and abiding by Peace Corps policies and procedures. Serving safely and effectively in Guatemala will require that you accept some restrictions on your current lifestyle.

Before and during service, your training will address these areas of concern so you can reduce the risks you face. For example, here are some strategies Volunteers employ:

Strategies to reduce the risk/impact of burglary:

- Living with a local family or on a family compound (Please note: a 27-month homestay is mandatory in Guatemala)
- Put strong locks on doors and keep valuables in a lock box or trunk
- Leave irreplaceable objects at home in the U.S.
- Purchase the Peace Corps-recommended personal property insurance
- Follow Peace Corps guidelines on maintaining home security

Strategies to reduce the risk/impact of assault:

- Make friends with local people who are respected in the community
- Make sure your appearance is respectful of local customs; don't draw negative attention to yourself by wearing inappropriate clothing
- Get to know local officials, police, and neighbors
- Travel with someone trusted by your community whenever possible and only on Peace Corps-approved transportation
- Avoid known high-crime areas
- Limit alcohol consumption

Support from Staff

If a trainee or Volunteer is the victim of a safety incident, Peace Corps staff is prepared to provide support. All Peace Corps posts have procedures in place to respond to incidents of crime committed against Volunteers. The first priority for all posts in the aftermath of an incident is to ensure the Volunteer is safe and receiving medical treatment as needed. After assuring the safety of the Volunteer, Peace Corps staff response may include reassessing the Volunteer's worksite and housing arrangements and making any adjustments, as needed. In some cases, the nature of the incident may necessitate a site or housing transfer. Peace Corps staff will also assist Volunteers with preserving their rights to pursue legal sanctions against the perpetrators of the crime. It is very important that Volunteers report incidents as they occur, not only to protect their peer Volunteers, but also to preserve the future right to prosecute. Should Volunteers decide later in the process that they want to proceed with the prosecution of their assailant, this option may no longer exist if the evidence of the event has not been preserved at the time of the incident.

Crime Data for Guatemala

Crime data and statistics for Guatemala, which is updated yearly, are available at the following link: http://www.peacecorps.gov/countrydata/guatemala. Please take the time to review this important information.

Few Peace Corps Volunteers are victims of serious crimes and crimes that do occur overseas are investigated and prosecuted by local authorities through the local courts system. If you are the victim of a crime, you will decide if you wish to pursue prosecution. If you decide to prosecute, Peace Corps will be there to assist you. One of our tasks is to ensure you are fully informed of your options and understand how the local legal process works. Peace Corps will help you ensure your rights are protected to the fullest extent possible under the laws of the country.

If you are the victim of a serious crime, you will learn how to get to a safe location as quickly as possible and contact your Peace Corps office. It's important that you notify Peace Corps as soon as you can so Peace Corps can provide you with the help you need.

Volunteer Safety Support in Guatemala

The Peace Corps' approach to safety is a five-pronged plan to help you stay safe during your service and includes the following: information sharing, Volunteer training, site selection criteria, a detailed emergency action plan, and protocols for addressing safety and security incidents. Guatemala's in-country safety program is outlined below.

The Peace Corps/Guatemala office will keep you informed of any issues that may impact Volunteer safety through **information sharing**. Regular updates will be provided in Volunteer newsletters and in memorandums from the country director. In the event of a critical situation or emergency, you will be contacted through the emergency communication network. An important component of the capacity of Peace Corps to keep you informed is your buy-in to the partnership concept with the Peace Corps staff. It is expected that you will do your part in ensuring that Peace Corps staff members are kept apprised of your travel in-country so they are able to inform you of any emergency.

Volunteer training will include sessions on specific safety and security issues in Guatemala. This training will prepare you to adopt a culturally appropriate lifestyle and exercise judgment that promotes safety and reduces risk in your home, at work, and while traveling. Safety training is offered throughout service and is integrated into the language, cross-cultural aspects, health, and other components of training. You will be expected to successfully complete all training competencies in a variety of areas, including safety and security, as a condition of service.

Certain **site selection criteria** are used to determine safe housing for Volunteers before their arrival. The Peace Corps staff works closely with host communities, host families, and counterpart agencies to help prepare them for a Volunteer's arrival and to establish expectations of their respective roles in supporting the Volunteer. Each site is inspected before the Volunteer's arrival to ensure placement in appropriate, safe, and secure housing and worksites. Site selection is based, in part, on any relevant site history; access to medical, banking, postal, and other essential services; availability of communications, transportation, and markets; different housing options and living arrangements; and other Volunteer support needs.

You will also learn about Peace Corps/Guatemala's **detailed emergency action plan,** which is implemented in the event of civil or political unrest or a natural disaster. When you arrive at your site, you will complete and submit a site locator form with your address, contact information, and a map to your house. If there is a security threat, you will gather with other Volunteers in Guatemala at predetermined locations until the situation is resolved or the Peace Corps decides to evacuate.

Finally, in order for the Peace Corps to be fully responsive to the needs of Volunteers, it is imperative that Volunteers immediately report any security incident to the Peace Corps office. The Peace Corps has established **protocols for addressing safety and security incidents** in a timely and appropriate manner, and it collects and evaluates safety and security data to track trends and develop strategies to minimize risks to future Volunteers.

DIVERSITY AND CROSS-CULTURAL ISSUES

In fulfilling its mandate to share the face of America with host countries, the Peace Corps is making special efforts to assure that all of America's richness is reflected in the Volunteer corps. More Americans of color are serving in today's Peace Corps than at any time in recent history. Differences in race, ethnic background, age, religion, and sexual orientation are expected and welcomed among our Volunteers. Part of the Peace Corps' mission is to help dispel any notion that Americans are all of one origin or race and to establish that each of us is as thoroughly American as the other despite our many differences.

Our diversity helps us accomplish that goal. In other ways, however, it poses challenges. In Guatemala, as in other Peace Corps host countries, Volunteers' behavior, lifestyle, background, and beliefs are judged in a cultural context very different from their own. Certain personal perspectives or characteristics commonly accepted in the United States may be quite uncommon, unacceptable, or even repressed in Guatemala.

Outside of Guatemala's capital, residents of rural communities have had relatively little direct exposure to other cultures, races, religions, and lifestyles. What people view as typical American behavior or norms may be a misconception, such as the belief that all Americans are rich and have blond hair and blue eyes. The people of Guatemala are justly known for their generous hospitality to foreigners; however, members of the community in which you will live may display a range of reactions to cultural differences that you present.

To ease the transition and adapt to life in Guatemala, you may need to make some temporary, yet fundamental compromises in how you present yourself as an American and as an individual. For example, female trainees and Volunteers may not be able to exercise the independence available to them in the United States; political discussions need to be handled with great care; and some of your personal beliefs may best remain undisclosed. You will need to develop techniques and personal strategies for coping with these and other limitations. The Peace Corps staff will lead diversity and sensitivity discussions during pre-service training and will be on call to provide support, but the challenge ultimately will be your own.

Overview of Diversity in Guatemala

The Peace Corps staff in Guatemala recognizes the adjustment issues that come with diversity and will endeavor to provide support and guidance. During pre-service training, several sessions will be held to discuss diversity and coping strategies. We look forward to having male and female Volunteers from a variety of races, ethnic groups, ages, religions, and sexual orientations, and hope that you will become part of a diverse group of Americans who take pride in supporting one another and demonstrating the richness of American culture.

In the past, Peace Corps/Guatemala has had an active diversity network. The diversity network has worked with several goals in mind, including, but not limited to, open communication, common ground building, and acceptance training. Currently, the Gender and Development (GAD) and the Cultural, Ethnic and Diversity Development groups have developed a co-facilitated, interactive, and thought provoking training session that focuses on group dynamics, stereotypes, and discrimination. This group of Volunteers is currently working with Peace Corps/Guatemala staff to encourage dialogue as a way to address and embrace our differences as Americans.

What Might a Volunteer Face?

Possible Issues for Female Volunteers

In rural Guatemala, there is a genuine division between the roles of women and those of men. The degree of separation frequently leads people to rely on stereotypical beliefs about people of the opposite sex—men with respect to women and vice versa. This dependence upon stereotypical images lends itself to the dehumanization of relations between men and women and to a situation in which people are viewed as objects. Unfortunately, the image of American women portrayed in many popular television programs suggests that they are sexually available. Additionally, in some regions of Guatemala, male virility is identified with power and social dominance. Many female Volunteers find the numerous sexually explicit invitations they receive to be intolerable and offensive. However, during pre-service training, Peace Corps/Guatemala staff and Volunteers will help trainees develop appropriate and effective strategies to deal with these issues.

Possible Issues for Volunteers of Color

The dynamic of racism does not play out in Guatemala in quite the same way as it does in the United States. The first identification of the Volunteer is as a *gringo*, an identification that is a mixture of admiration and resentment that varies from person to person. *Gringos* are typically thought of as being of Caucasian descent, rich, and sometimes overbearing. Therefore, Volunteers of color are often not initially viewed as *gringos* or even American. Stereotypically, all Asian Americans are described as *chino* and sometimes are assumed to be associated with the Korean clothing industry present in Guatemala. African Americans are called *moreno* or *negro* and often are thought to be *garifuna*, a Guatemalan ethnic group primarily populating the Caribbean coast. Volunteers of Latin and Southeast Asian descent are often assumed to be Guatemalan. Conversations with Guatemalans regarding one's ethnicity and heritage are numerous, sometimes to the point of being annoying. However, this allows Volunteers the opportunity to educate host country nationals about the true nature of American diversity. Without a doubt, Volunteers of color have positive, rich, and successful Peace Corps experiences in Guatemala.

Volunteer Comment

"It's nice to know that everywhere I go in Guatemala, people are interested in knowing who I am and what I represent as an American. As a person of color, I am more than just an American volunteer; I am a representative of the diversity that makes America so unique."

Possible Issues for Senior Volunteers

Senior Volunteers may feel they have successfully resolved many challenges of holding down a job, establishing relationships, and perhaps even raising a family. In Guatemala, they might find that the "big questions" to which they have the "answers" are different from the ones in the United States. Also, learning a second language is tough at any age. Some senior Volunteers have expressed that it may take a little longer than it might have when they were younger. An additional challenge can be the lack of amenities taken for granted in the U.S., so it's good to be prepared to be flexible, such as, enjoying warm bucket baths instead of showers. Most of your fellow Volunteers will be considerably younger, and their idealism and energy is inspiring. At times, there can be a desire to interact with those closer in age to your own, so staff members at the Peace Corps office can often help provide that social connection. Overall, in Guatemala seniors are treated with great respect and this works in the favor of senior Volunteers.

Volunteer Comments

"Guatemala is a country where most of the population is younger than 20 years old. Babies, toddlers, and young children seem to be almost everywhere. A person in his or her 40s in a rural community is traditionally considered to be an elder, and tends to be afforded a good deal of deference and respect. Senior Volunteers will often find themselves adopted as 'honorary grandparents' for much of the community."

"On the other hand, most young villagers believe that elders are no longer interested, or able to play a role in the work of a community or village. However, with a sense of humor you can figure out how far you can go in offering advice and suggestions. Learning Spanish is hard work, but if you keep trying, it will come. In the meantime, the few words you know, along with gestures and a smile, will go a long way."

"Routine medical care in larger cities is good and the Peace Corps medical staff is outstanding. Living out in the countryside is a little more complicated, but on my trips to more urban areas, I stock up on items I can't buy at home. Getting around is always an adventure, and public transportation is very inexpensive."

"I have experienced a deference that is not always accorded to elderly Guatemalans, so when someone kindly offers a seat on the bus, I acknowledge the kind gesture and gladly accept! It's rewarding to be an example of the challenges we can undertake, no matter what our age. Through our presence here, we demonstrate the diversity of Americans, especially as Volunteers. It definitely impresses people that we chose to leave behind loved ones to live in their country for two years."

Possible Issues for Gay, Lesbian, or Bisexual Volunteers

In Guatemala, the common perception of same-sex couples is different than that in the United States. Same-sex relationships are considered by many to be taboo and can provoke varied reactions in rural communities. Neighbors and friends in rural communities may deny the existence of homosexuality within their community, believing it to only exist in the capital and in other countries. For Volunteers, there is pressure to live more "in" than "out," especially in rural communities, despite having been "out" in the United States.

Lesbians, as most women in general, will have to deal with constant questions about boyfriends, marriage, and sex. Gay men must deal with *machismo*: talk of sexual conquests, girl watching, and dirty jokes.

Most tourist destinations have a more relaxed attitude, and discrete homosexuality is less likely to provoke a severe reaction as in village communities.

Despite generally negative perceptions of homosexuality within Guatemala, there are openly gay Guatemalans, as well as some gay organizations and businesses that serve and advocate for the LGBT community, especially in the capital and Quetzaltenango and in some tourist areas. In addition, an LGBT committee of Volunteers provides support for trainees and Volunteers, and periodically organizes social outings for gay, lesbian, bisexual, and transgender Volunteers and friends. Peace Corps/Guatemala staff is available and enthusiastic to support Volunteers' initiative in renewing this group.

Volunteer Comment

"Guatemala has many contrasts. The perspective toward homosexuality is one of them. Although in most areas the issue of homosexuality is negatively viewed, there are stark differences in how one manages life as a gay Volunteer. In the *oriente* (east), one has to deal with rampant sexist and homophobic jokes, while in the *altiplano* (highlands), the Mayan culture has traditionally been more tolerant, at least overtly. Still, in the altiplano, one has to manage other issues. With patience, professionalism, and humor, virtually all issues related to homosexuality can be assuaged.

"Like everywhere, gay folks have managed to find their niche in Guatemalan society. This tends to be most likely in the capital, in Quetzaltenango, and in tourist areas. Although living a closeted life in rural Guatemala can be lonely, there are always other Volunteers, foreigners, and Guatemalans to provide a necessary social outlet."

Possible Religious Issues for Volunteers

Guatemala is a profoundly religious country where religion is public and emotional. For Volunteers used to a more contemplative or low-key religious tradition, it may be a challenge to identify other people who can support your faith. Although Guatemala's constitution guarantees freedom of religion, most churches are either Roman Catholic or Christian Fundamentalist. In the tension between Catholics and Fundamentalists, there has been little recognition of other faith communities, including Mayan religious practices, but this is changing. Many Guatemalans remain uninformed about Judaism. Managing a conversation can be delicate and some Volunteers have had difficulty being open about their Jewish ethnicity. There is, however, a rich history of Jews in Guatemala and an active Jewish community that welcomes foreigners. There are also various Christian denominations, and Hindu and Muslim communities in Guatemala. Peace Corps/Guatemala staff can provide information to Volunteers who are interested in connecting to various communities of faith.

Possible Issues for Volunteers with Disabilities

As part of the medical clearance process, the Peace Corps Office of Medical Services determined that you were physically and emotionally capable, with or without reasonable accommodations, to perform a full tour of Volunteer service in Guatemala without unreasonable risk of harm to yourself or interruption of service. The Peace Corps/ Guatemala staff will work with disabled Volunteers to make reasonable accommodations for them in training, housing, jobsites, or other areas to enable them to serve safely and effectively.

In the wake of 36 years of civil war, there are a number of people with permanent disabilities. However, there is virtually no consideration for access to public transportation or public buildings for persons with disabilities.

Possible Issues for Married Volunteers

Married couples may face unique challenges in Guatemala. For instance, a married man may be encouraged to be the more dominant member in the relationship. He may also be encouraged by the local culture to make decisions independent of his spouse's views and to have his wife serve him. He may be ridiculed if he performs domestic tasks. On the other hand, a married woman may find herself in a less independent role than that to which she has been accustomed. In addition, it may be common for community leaders to address the man during official matters, even in the event that the woman may be the one spearheading an event.

Couples may also experience a more limited social life in the community than single Volunteers (since it may be assumed that the woman will be busy taking care of her husband). Additionally, female married PCVs may be expected by the local culture to perform "traditional" domestic chores, such as cooking or cleaning. Competition between the couple may become a difficulty, especially if one spouse learns faster than the other (e.g., language skills, job skills). There might be differences in job satisfaction and/or different needs between spouses. Younger Volunteers may look to couples for advice and support. Married couples also are likely to be treated with more respect because the community sees marriage as a responsibility. They may be asked when they will have children.

Depending on the age of the couple, social interaction with other married couples may be very uncommon because of social norms. This is due to the fact that the majority of young couples quickly begin to have children and/or engage in domestic tasks and tend to focus on those priorities rather than socializing. Culturally, men tend to socialize much more with other men than women so the husband may find more social outlets than the woman.

Please note: Married couples will likely not live together during pre-service training (PST). The community-based training model locates trainees in communities based on their technical program and Spanish level. Special considerations are given to couples so that they live in nearby communities, and they will have more flexibility to see each other. Language acquisition and cultural integration increase when each member of the couple has a separate host family. The couple will serve together in the same site for the two years of their Volunteer service.

FREQUENTLY ASKED QUESTIONS

Below are answers to some of the most frequently asked questions that can help you prepare for your upcoming departure.

How much luggage am I allowed to bring to Guatemala?
Most airlines have baggage size and weight limits and assess charges for transport of baggage that exceeds those limits. The Peace Corps has its own size and weight limits and will not pay the cost of transport for baggage that exceeds these limits. The Peace Corps' allowance is two checked pieces of luggage with combined dimensions of both pieces not to exceed 107 inches (length + width + height) and a carry-on bag with dimensions of no more than 45 inches. Checked baggage should not exceed 100 pounds total with a maximum weight of 50 pounds for any one bag.

This policy does not mean that you aren't allowed more than 100 pounds of luggage, but that you will be responsible for any potential charges for amounts over that weight. Questions about baggage limits should be directed to the particular domestic and international airlines on which you will be traveling. The Peace Corps recommends you do not bring more than you can carry. You will be responsible for handling your luggage en route to post and overseas.

If you exceed an airline's baggage limits, you may be assessed a fee. However, if your luggage conforms to the parameters stated above, the Peace Corps will reimburse you for fees incurred for which you have a valid receipt.

Peace Corps Volunteers are not allowed to take pets, weapons, explosives, radio transmitters (shortwave radios are permitted), automobiles, or motorcycles to their overseas assignments. Do not pack flammable materials or liquids such as lighter fluid, cleaning solvents, hair spray, or aerosol containers. This is an important safety precaution.

Please check the Transportation Security Administration (TSA) website for a detailed list of permitted and prohibited items at http://www.tsa.gov/travelers/airtravel/prohibited/permitted-prohibited-items.shtm.

What is the electric current in Guatemala?
Electric current is the U.S. standard 120 volts.

How much money should I bring?
Volunteers are expected to live at the same level as the people in their community. You will be given a settling-in allowance and a monthly living allowance, which should cover your expenses. Volunteers often wish to bring additional money for vacation travel to other countries. Credit cards and traveler's checks are preferable to cash. If you do bring cash, please ensure that the bills are crisp and without defects. If you choose to bring extra money, bring the amount that will suit your own travel plans and needs.

When can I take vacation and have people visit me?
Each Volunteer accrues two vacation days per month of service (excluding training). Leave may not be taken during training, the first three months of service, or the last three months of service, except in conjunction with an authorized emergency leave. Family and friends are welcome to visit you after pre-service training and the first three months of service as long as their stay does not interfere with your work. Extended stays at your site are not encouraged and require permission from your country director. The Peace Corps is not able to provide your visitors with visa, medical, or travel assistance.

Will my belongings be covered by insurance?

The Peace Corps does not provide insurance coverage for personal effects; Volunteers are ultimately responsible for the safekeeping of their personal belongings. However, you can purchase personal property insurance before you leave. If you wish, you may contact your own insurance company; additionally, insurance application forms will be provided, and we encourage you to consider them carefully. Volunteers should not ship or take valuable items overseas. Jewelry, watches, radios, cameras, and expensive appliances are subject to loss, theft, and breakage, and in many places, satisfactory maintenance and repair services are not available.

Do I need an international driver's license?

Volunteers in Guatemala do not need an international driver's license because they are prohibited from operating privately owned motorized vehicles. Most urban travel is by bus or taxi. Rural travel ranges from buses and minibuses to trucks, bicycles, and plenty of walking.

What should I bring as gifts for Guatemalan friends and my host family?

This is not a requirement. A token of friendship is sufficient. Some gift suggestions include knickknacks for the house, pictures, books, and calendars, souvenirs from your hometown, hard candies that will not melt or spoil, or photos to give away. Photos of your family are also great conversation pieces.

Where will my site assignment be when I finish training and how isolated will I be?

Peace Corps trainees are not assigned to individual sites until after they have completed pre-service training. This gives Peace Corps staff the opportunity to assess each trainee's technical and language skills prior to assigning sites, in addition to finalizing site selections with their ministry counterparts. If feasible, you may have the opportunity to provide input on your site preferences, including geographical location, distance from other Volunteers, and living conditions. However, keep in mind that many factors influence the site selection process and that the Peace Corps cannot guarantee placement according to personalized preferences. Most Volunteers live in small towns or in rural villages and are usually within one hour from another Volunteer. Some sites are located 10 to 12 hours from the capital. There are also Volunteers in municipal and regional capitals.

How can my family contact me in an emergency?

The Peace Corps' Counseling and Outreach Unit (COU) provides assistance in handling emergencies affecting trainees and Volunteers or their families. Before leaving the United States, instruct your family to notify the COU immediately if an emergency arises, such as a serious illness or death of a family member. During normal business hours, the number for the Counseling and Outreach Unit is 1-855-855-1961, then press 2; or directly at 202-692-1470. For non-emergency questions, your family can get information from your country desk staff at the Peace Corps by calling 1-855-855-1961, press 1 for the staff directory, and then extension 2521. The Guatemala desk can also be reached via email at Guatemala@peacecorps.gov.

Can I call home from Guatemala?

Virtually all PCVs make long-distance international calls from their own cellular phones using pre-paid telephone cards widely available around the country. Calls to the U.S. under most cellphone plans cost less than 15 cents per minute. Most Volunteers use the Internet for non-emergency international communications.

Should I bring a cellular phone with me?

During pre-service training, all Peace Corps trainees are assigned a cellular phone for use during their service, which must be returned upon completing service. Calls to staff members, the Peace Corps office, and other trainees and Volunteers are free using the Peace Corps-issued phone. Each phone also comes with minutes every month to make calls and send text messages, local or international. Volunteers can add minutes to their cellular phones in local shops to use for local or international calls. Phones brought from the U.S. may not be compatible with local networks so it is generally advisable to use your Peace Corps phone.

Will there be email and Internet access? Should I bring my computer?

Email and Internet access are available in most of the country, either in Internet cafes (where computer terminals can be rented by the hour) or through the purchase of a modem and Internet time, either on an hourly, weekly, or monthly basis. During training, you will have sporadic access to Internet depending on your training town. There are, however, several Volunteer workstations in the Peace Corps office that you can use to check your email once a week.

It is your decision whether to bring a laptop. Volunteers who choose to bring their laptops generally use them to create documents for work-related purposes, check email, or communicate with friends and family back home. It is important to know that laptops bring a good price in the local markets for stolen goods so they are at some risk of being stolen. In order to minimize risk, it is advisable to avoid traveling with laptops or other electronics on public transportation and keep them secured in your home when not in use. In the last two years, many Volunteers have chosen to purchase Netbook-style laptops, which are smaller and less expensive. Peace Corps cannot reimburse Volunteers for damage or theft to laptops or other electronic devices and advises Volunteers to seriously consider property insurance. Please remember that the Peace Corps is unable to provide you with hardware or software assistance for a personal laptop and it is up to you to maintain it if you bring it.

WELCOME LETTERS FROM
GUATEMALA VOLUNTEERS

Dear Prospective Peace Corps Volunteers of Guatemala,

Congratulations and welcome to a remarkable experience! Guatemala is a country rich in culture and history, with a plethora of indigenous languages, spectacular volcanoes and scenery, and most of all, a wholesome communal feel. Communities in which we live and work need enthused Volunteers who are eager to develop joint relationships of learning and cultural exchange.

I am thoroughly enjoying my primary work of teaching life skills in the youth development project, and have acquired a refreshed passion for developing need-based projects. Thus far, one of the best moments of my service involves collaborating with a girls group through an international nonprofit organization to create community tire gardens. The gardens introduced sustainable food development, environmental care, and were even publicized in press releases. I have since held sports tournaments to introduce young girls to tennis, volleyball, and baseball with equipment donated from a youth sports organization.

The opportunities to be a change agent are endless. Your service is undeniably what you make of it and can be rewarding if you come in with an open mind, a sense of humor, and lots of patience and flexibility. Always remember, development work is extraordinary, but not without its challenges! I wish you the very best in enjoying the toughest job you'll ever love!

Keisha Kailua Herbert (2010-2013)

Dear Prospective Peace Corps Volunteers of Guatemala,

Congratulations on being invited to serve with Peace Corps/Guatemala! You are one step closer to embarking on an experience of a lifetime. At this moment, you're most likely feeling a weight lift from your shoulders now that the application process is winding down. Your fears and anxieties will eventually return and you'll be wondering what is truly ahead of you. I recommend taking this time to relax and take pride in the fact you're about to join a big supportive family.

Over a year into my service, I can assure you that my job as a healthy homes Volunteer has truly been life changing. Sanitary conditions in the rural areas are poor and contribute to high mortality rates. Diarrhea and respiratory illnesses are the main culprits and the chance to improve rural heath by teaching and visiting communities is very fulfilling. The women in my health promoter groups are some of the most hard-working and inspirational individuals I have ever met. The relationships you form and the lives you impact are limitless. Also, some of the greatest accomplishments of Volunteers can take the form of secondary projects, and I am confident you'll find opportunities and make a positive difference.

The Peace Corps can be intimidating, but know that with patience, flexibility, and creativity, you can definitely achieve great things. In looking forward, I realize the remaining year of my service is going to fly by really fast. There is so much to do and see. The Guatemalans and the Volunteers around you will shape your life, not only during your service, but in years to come. On behalf of Volunteers before me and those currently serving: Welcome to Guatemala! You're about to join and help grow an incredible legacy.

Jacob Brennan (2011-2013)

PACKING LIST

This list has been compiled by Volunteers serving in Guatemala and is based on their experience. Use it as an informal guide in making your own list, bearing in mind that each experience is individual. There is no perfect list! You obviously cannot bring everything on the list, so consider those items that make the most sense to you personally and professionally. You can always have things sent to you later. As you decide what to bring, keep in mind that you have a 100-pound weight limit on baggage. And remember, you can get almost everything you need in Guatemala.

The climate in Guatemala varies greatly from cold to hot. The Peace Corps office in Santa Lucia Milpas Altas (near Antigua) is at a high altitude. Therefore, it can be very cold at night and in the training rooms during the morning hours. It can be quite cold for the training group that arrives in February, and quite rainy for the group that arrives later in the calendar year. Furthermore, the majority of Volunteers are placed in sites in the western highlands, where high altitudes lead to cold temperatures, especially November through February. It cannot be stressed enough that although the prevailing image of a Central American country is of sun-soaked beaches and palm trees (those areas exist in Guatemala, but there are no Volunteer sites on the beach and a very small number in warm climates), the mountainous terrain of Guatemala can produce very cold temperatures. Keep this in mind when packing and prefer layers of clothing.

General Clothing

- One or two pairs of nice pants (lightweight that dry quickly can be helpful)

- Two to four pairs of work pants or jeans

- Four T-shirts or short-sleeve polo shirts

- Two or three blouses or dress shirts

- Two-week supply of underwear and socks

- One pair of long underwear

- One pair of wool socks

- One or two medium-weight sweaters/sweatshirts

- One medium-weight jacket or fleece

- One raincoat

For Men
- A tie, one or two nice dress shirts, and a sport coat (optional) for formal occasions like the swearing-in ceremony.

For Women
- Two casual dresses

- One "dress-up" dress

- One or two "going-out" outfits

- One or two knee-length skirts

- PJ pants or comfy sweats for the house

- Scarf

Other Clothing Items
- Belt

- Handkerchiefs

- Running or athletic gear (if you are into sports)

- Swimming suit

- Two hats (sun hats, visors, or caps with bill)

- One cold-weather cap

- One pair of lightweight gloves

- Sunglasses

Note: The general characteristics for clothes are sturdy, easily washable, iron-free (if possible), and conservative. Bring what you are comfortable wearing, such as presentable items you might wear on a weekend in the U.S. You do not need to change your whole style because you are a Volunteer. Good quality, used clothes are also available in many Guatemalan markets or stores (called *Ropa Americana*).

Additionally, many Volunteers have noted their work often requires business casual for special meetings or events. As one Volunteer noted, "Although many items on this list may seem like it, you are **not preparing** for a two-year camping trip, nor do you need to."

Shoes
- One or two pairs of sturdy walking, tennis, or cross-training shoes (waterproof tennis shoes are preferable)
- One pair of hiking boots or waterproof shoes
- One to two pairs of comfortable casual/dress shoes (closed-toed)
- One pair of shower flip-flops
- One pair of farm/mud boots or rain boots

Note: The overall selection and quality of shoes in Guatemala is more limited than in the United States. It is difficult to find women's shoes larger than size 9 and men's shoes larger than size 10. If you have larger feet, you may want to consider a plan for getting extra shoes once the ones you bring wear out (e.g., bring a two-year supply, have people bring you shoes when they come to visit, or arrange for people to send them to you).

Personal Hygiene and Toiletry Items

- Your regular hygiene items (e.g., soap, shampoo, shaving cream, etc.) to get you started (replacements/refills are easily purchased here)

- Three-month supply of prescription medicine

- Extra pair of prescription glasses

- Refillable travel-size shampoo/soap containers

- One bath towel and quick-dry towel for traveling

Note: Each trainee will receive a "Medical Kit" stocked full of useful items soon after arriving, and Peace Corps medical staff will supply you with over-the-counter medicines such as vitamins, painkillers, cold medicines, Tampax-brand tampons, etc. throughout your service.

Miscellaneous

- Sturdy backpack/duffel bag for three- or four-day trips

- Day pack/small backpack

- Laptop computer (if you can't live without one in the U.S., then you probably won't want to live without one here)

- Music (MP3 players and travel-size speakers are a good idea if you are bringing audio equipment, and CDs are sold in every market at very cheap prices)

- USB storage stick

- Digital camera (free online photo sites are convenient places to store photos for those without a personal computer or you may want to bring a few blank CDs to transfer your photos during training)

- Flashlight (headlamps are popular)

- Watch (fairly cheap and water-resistant/proof)

- Small travel alarm clock

- Money belt or pouch that fits under your clothes for your passport, money, and/or a wallet or change purse to carry small amounts of money

- One sturdy water bottle

- Pocketknife (basic knife, corkscrew, screwdriver model is very handy)

- Sleeping bag

- Sleeping pad

- Waterproof cases for cameras , MP3 players, or other electronic devices

- Earplugs for sleeping (Guatemala can be a very loud country and although Peace Corps does have earplugs to distribute, they are not very comfortable to wear while sleeping)

- Travel guide to Guatemala

- Small, basic cookbook or favorite recipes (Peace Corps/Guatemala also publishes *"Qué Rico!"* a cookbook of Volunteer-compiled recipes that are easily prepared with common items sold at markets)

- Photos of family, friends, and home (Guatemalans will love to see your photos)

- Decks of cards and a travel-sized version of your favorite board game

- Small sewing kit

- Duct tape

- Instrument (if you play one)

- Books (Peace Corps has a fairly large library at the training center with books passed down from Volunteers)

- Start-up supply of stationery, pens, journal, etc.

- One set of flat sheets and pillow cases for a full bed

- Comfort foods (favorite snack foods)

Tips & Notes:

- Guatemala uses the same 120 voltage current as in the United States; therefore, any appliance or charger from the U.S. will work here. Also, the plug-ins and sockets are the same, but the majority of them only accept two prongs. Two- to three-prong converters can be found here, but it might be better to bring MP3 chargers, blow dryers, computer cords, etc. that are two-pronged or bring an adapter with you.

- Anything you bring, especially the more expensive items, has the possibility of being lost, stolen, or damaged. The Peace Corps is not responsible for personal items, so you might want to consider insurance for items that would be costly to be replaced.

- As mentioned in this packing list, you can find practically everything you need here in Guatemala. *Paiz* and Walmart stores (large discount goods or department stores) are located in most of the major cities. While the selection of items in your site most certainly won't be as vast, there is a large quantity of familiar American brands of clothing, toiletry items, food, electronics, etc. available in Guatemala.

PRE-DEPARTURE CHECKLIST

The following list consists of suggestions for you to consider as you prepare to live outside the United States for two years. Not all items will be relevant to everyone, and the list does not include everything you should make arrangements for.

Family
- Notify family that they can call the Peace Corps' Counseling and Outreach Unit at any time if there is a critical illness or death of a family member (24-hour telephone number: 855-855-1961, then press 2; or directly at 202-692-1470).

- Give the Peace Corps' *On the Home Front* handbook to family and friends.

Passport/Travel
- Forward to the Peace Corps travel office all paperwork for the Peace Corps passport and visas.

- Verify that your luggage meets the size and weight limits for international travel.

- Obtain a personal passport if you plan to travel after your service ends. (Your Peace Corps passport will expire three months after you finish your service, so if you plan to travel longer, you will need a regular passport.)

Medical/Health
- Complete any needed dental and medical work.

- If you wear glasses, bring two pairs.

- Arrange to bring a three-month supply of all medications (including birth control pills) you are currently taking.

Insurance
- Make arrangements to maintain life insurance coverage.

- Arrange to maintain supplemental health coverage while you are away. (Even though the Peace Corps is responsible for your health care during Peace Corps service overseas, it is advisable for people who have pre-existing conditions to arrange for the continuation of their supplemental health coverage. If there is a lapse in coverage, it is often difficult and expensive to be reinstated.)

- Arrange to continue Medicare coverage if applicable.

Personal Papers
- Bring a copy of your certificate of marriage or divorce.

Voting
- Register to vote in the state of your home of record. (Many state universities consider voting and payment of state taxes as evidence of residence in that state.)

- Obtain a voter registration card and take it with you overseas.

- Arrange to have an absentee ballot forwarded to you overseas.

Personal Effects

- Purchase personal property insurance to extend from the time you leave your home for service overseas until the time you complete your service and return to the United States.

Financial Management

- Keep a bank account in your name in the U.S.

- Obtain student loan deferment forms from the lender or loan service.

- Execute a Power of Attorney for the management of your property and business.

- Arrange for deductions from your readjustment allowance to pay alimony, child support, and other debts through the Office of Volunteer Financial Operations at 855.855.1961, extension 1770.

- Place all important papers—mortgages, deeds, stocks, and bonds—in a safe deposit box or with an attorney or other caretaker.

CONTACTING PEACE CORPS HEADQUARTERS

This list of numbers will help connect you with the appropriate office at Peace Corps headquarters to answer various questions. You can use the toll-free number and extension or dial directly using the local numbers provided. Be sure to leave the toll-free number and extensions with your family so they can contact you in the event of an emergency.

Peace Corps Headquarters Toll-free Number: 855-855-1961

Peace Corps' Mailing Address: Peace Corps
Paul D. Coverdell Peace Corps Headquarters
1111 20th Street, NW
Washington, DC 20526

For Questions About:	Staff:	Toll-Free Ext:	Direct/Local Number:
Responding to an Invitation:	Office of Placement	x1840	202.692.1840
Country Information	Michael McGuire	x2521	202.692.2521
	Desk Officer / GuatemalaDesk@peacecorps.gov		

Plane Tickets, Passports, Visas, or other travel matters:

	CWT SATO Travel	x1170	202.692.1170
Legal Clearance	Office of Placement	x1845	202.692.1840

Medical Clearance and Forms Processing (includes dental):

	Screening Nurse	x1500	202.692.1500
Medical Reimbursements (handled by a subcontractor)			800.818.8772
Loan Deferments, Taxes, Financial Operations		x1770	202.692.1770

Readjustment Allowance Withdrawals, Power of Attorney, Staging (Pre-Departure Orientation), and Reporting Instructions:

	Office of Staging	x1865	202.692.1865

Note: You will receive comprehensive information (hotel and flight arrangements three to five weeks prior to departure. This information is not available sooner.

Family Emergencies (to get information to a Volunteer overseas) *24 hours:*

	Counseling and Outreach Unit	x1470	202.692.1470

www.ingramcontent.com/pod-product-compliance
Lightning Source LLC
Chambersburg PA
CBHW080348290526
45791CB00009BA/2792